MAD  LIBS®

I LOVE SEATTLE MAD LIBS

concept created by Roger Price & Leonard S

PSS!

PRICE STERN SLOAN

An Imprint of Penguin Group (USA) LLC

PRICE STERN SLOAN
Published by the Penguin Group
Penguin Group (USA) LLC, 375 Hudson Street, New York, New York 10014, USA

USA | Canada | UK | Ireland | Australia | New Zealand | India | South Africa | China

penguin.com
A Penguin Random House Company

Mad Libs format and text copyright © 2014 by Price Stern Sloan, an imprint of
Penguin Group (USA) LLC. All rights reserved.

Published by Price Stern Sloan, a division of Penguin Young Readers Group,
345 Hudson Street, New York, New York 10014.
Printed in the USA.

ISBN 978-0-8431-8268-2

1 3 5 7 9 10 8 6 4 2

PSS! and *MAD LIBS* are registered trademarks of Penguin Group (USA) LLC.

MAD LIBS
INSTRUCTIONS

MAD LIBS® is a game for people who don't like games!
It can be played by one, two, three, four, or forty.

• RIDICULOUSLY SIMPLE DIRECTIONS

In this tablet you will find stories containing blank spaces where words are left out. One player, the READER, selects one of these stories. The READER does not tell anyone what the story is about. Instead, he/she asks the other players, the WRITERS, to give him/her words. These words are used to fill in the blank spaces in the story.

• TO PLAY

The READER asks each WRITER in turn to call out a word—an adjective or a noun or whatever the space calls for—and uses them to fill in the blank spaces in the story. The result is a MAD LIBS® game.

When the READER then reads the completed MAD LIBS® game to the other players, they will discover that they have written a story that is fantastic, screamingly funny, shocking, silly, crazy, or just plain dumb—depending upon which words each WRITER called out.

• EXAMPLE (*Before* and *After*)

"_____!" he said _____
        EXCLAMATION   ADVERB

as he jumped into his convertible _____ and
                                            NOUN

drove off with his _____ wife.
                          ADJECTIVE

"_____*Ouch*_____!" he said _____*stupidly*_____
        EXCLAMATION   ADVERB

as he jumped into his convertible _____*cat*_____ and
                                            NOUN

drove off with his _____*brave*_____ wife.
                          ADJECTIVE

MAD LIBS®
QUICK REVIEW

In case you have forgotten what adjectives, adverbs, nouns, and verbs are, here is a quick review:

An ADJECTIVE describes something or somebody. *Lumpy, soft, ugly, messy,* and *short* are adjectives.

An ADVERB tells how something is done. It modifies a verb and usually ends in "ly." *Modestly, stupidly, greedily,* and *carefully* are adverbs.

A NOUN is the name of a person, place, or thing. *Sidewalk, umbrella, bridle, bathtub,* and *nose* are nouns.

A VERB is an action word. *Run, pitch, jump,* and *swim* are verbs. Put the verbs in past tense if the directions say PAST TENSE. *Ran, pitched, jumped,* and *swam* are verbs in the past tense.

When we ask for A PLACE, we mean any sort of place: a country or city (*Spain, Cleveland*) or a room (*bathroom, kitchen*).

An EXCLAMATION or SILLY WORD is any sort of funny sound, gasp, grunt, or outcry, like *Wow!, Ouch!, Whomp!, Ick!,* and *Gadzooks!*

When we ask for specific words, like a NUMBER, a COLOR, an ANIMAL, or a PART OF THE BODY, we mean a word that is one of those things, like *seven, blue, horse,* or *head.*

When we ask for a PLURAL, it means more than one. For example, *cat* pluralized is *cats.*

MAD LIBS® is fun to play with friends, but you can also play it by yourself! To begin with, DO NOT look at the story on the page below. Fill in the blanks on this page with the words called for. Then, using the words you have selected, fill in the blank spaces in the story.

Now you've created your own hilarious MAD LIBS® game!

WHAT'S IN A NAME?

PLURAL NOUN _____

ADJECTIVE _____

NOUN _____

NOUN _____

NOUN _____

NOUN _____

ADJECTIVE _____

NOUN _____

PLURAL NOUN _____

VERB _____

PLURAL NOUN _____

NOUN _____

ADJECTIVE _____

PERSON IN ROOM (FEMALE) _____

COLOR _____

ADJECTIVE _____

MAD LIBS®

WHAT'S IN A NAME?

_____ of Seattle, also known as Seattleites, have had several
　　PLURAL NOUN

_____ nicknames for their city over the years. Seattle's
　　ADJECTIVE

first nickname, "Queen _____ of the Pacific Northwest,"
　　　　　　　　　　　NOUN

was actually coined by a Portland-based real-estate _____
　　　　　　　　　　　　　　　　　　　　　　　　　　NOUN

in 1869. After the Klondike _____ Rush began in 1897,
　　　　　　　　　　　　　　　NOUN

Seattle declared itself the "_____ to Alaska." (Not sure
　　　　　　　　　　　　　　NOUN

how _____ that nickname is now.) In the 1950s, the tag
　　　ADJECTIVE

"Jet City" was often used for Seattle, thanks to _____
　　　　　　　　　　　　　　　　　　　　　　　　　NOUN

manufacturer Boeing. (However, the _____ living in
　　　　　　　　　　　　　　　　　PLURAL NOUN

Renton will _____ you over that nickname.) Beginning in
　　　　　　　VERB

1975, *Harper's Magazine* and other urban _____ dubbed
　　　　　　　　　　　　　　　　　　　　　PLURAL NOUN

Seattle "America's most livable _____," which soon became
　　　　　　　　　　　　　　　　NOUN

its _____ motto. And after a contest was held in 1982,
　　ADJECTIVE

the city's latest nickname became the Emerald City. But that name

has nothing to do with a wizard, _____, Toto, or
　　　　　　　　　　　　　　　PERSON IN ROOM (FEMALE)

_____ slippers. We all know that it's because Seattle is so
　COLOR

green from all the _____ rain it gets ALL.YEAR.ROUND.
　　　　　　　　　　ADJECTIVE

From I LOVE SEATTLE MAD LIBS® • Copyright © 2014 by Price Stern Sloan,
an imprint of Penguin Group (USA) LLC, 345 Hudson Street, New York, NY 10014.

MAD LIBS® is fun to play with friends, but you can also play it by yourself! To begin with, DO NOT look at the story on the page below. Fill in the blanks on this page with the words called for. Then, using the words you have selected, fill in the blank spaces in the story.

Now you've created your own hilarious MAD LIBS® game!

SEATTLE RUNS DRY!

ADJECTIVE _____

ADJECTIVE _____

ADJECTIVE _____

PLURAL NOUN _____

VERB ENDING IN "ING" _____

NOUN _____

ADVERB _____

ADJECTIVE _____

VERB (PAST TENSE) _____

PLURAL NOUN _____

OCCUPATION _____

TYPE OF LIQUID _____

ADJECTIVE _____

PLURAL NOUN _____

VERB _____

TYPE OF LIQUID _____

MAD LIBS

SEATTLE RUNS DRY!

News flash! In a/an _____ turn of events, Seattle has
ADJECTIVE

run dry of its favorite _____ beverage: coffee! Officials
ADJECTIVE

are questioning how such a/an _____ situation could
ADJECTIVE

have occurred, but in the meantime, _____ of Seattle
PLURAL NOUN

are _____ the city in droves. It is reported that
VERB ENDING IN "ING"

the city's _____ industry has been _____
NOUN   ADVERB

affected. Hotels are suffering a/an _____ number of
ADJECTIVE

cancellations, and airlines have _____ numerous flights
VERB (PAST TENSE)

into the city. (Meanwhile, _____ out of the city are
PLURAL NOUN

overbooked!) The head-_____ of one of Seattle's most
OCCUPATION

famous _____-houses has proclaimed this the most
TYPE OF LIQUID

_____ disaster in Seattle's history. What will the city and its
ADJECTIVE

_____ do without coffee? Will the city _____?
PLURAL NOUN   VERB

Or will it somehow make _____ the next big thing?
TYPE OF LIQUID

From I LOVE SEATTLE MAD LIBS® • Copyright © 2014 by Price Stern Sloan,
an imprint of Penguin Group (USA) LLC, 345 Hudson Street, New York, NY 10014.

MAD LIBS® is fun to play with friends, but you can also play it by yourself! To begin with, DO NOT look at the story on the page below. Fill in the blanks on this page with the words called for. Then, using the words you have selected, fill in the blank spaces in the story.

Now you've created your own hilarious MAD LIBS® game!

YOU GOT NOTHING ON ME

NOUN _____

ADJECTIVE _____

VERB _____

NUMBER _____

NOUN _____

ADJECTIVE _____

ADJECTIVE _____

PLURAL NOUN _____

ADJECTIVE _____

ADJECTIVE _____

OCCUPATION _____

ADJECTIVE _____

PERSON IN ROOM (FEMALE) _____

NOUN _____

PART OF THE BODY _____

ADJECTIVE _____

NOUN _____

MAD LIBS®

YOU GOT NOTHING ON ME

Hey, Empire State _____; Seattle Space Needle here. You
                          NOUN

think you're so _____—well, you don't _____
               ADJECTIVE   VERB

me. You may be taller (1,453 feet to my _____ feet), but
                                          NUMBER

I'm younger (you were built in 1931, while I was built for the 1962

World's _____), and I have a much more _____
        NOUN   ADJECTIVE

figure. Come on, you have to admit you are a bit straight up and down,

while I have got some _____ curves going on. Sure, you
                         ADJECTIVE

may have starred in hundreds of TV shows and _____,
                                          PLURAL NOUN

but I've had my _____ share of appearances on the small
                ADJECTIVE

and big screens. You don't believe me? Well, why don't you take a

look at the movies _____ in Seattle and *Austin Powers: The*
                  ADJECTIVE

_____ *Who Shagged Me*, and the _____ TV show
OCCUPATION   ADJECTIVE

for kids, *i-*_____. But let's not forget your spectacular
        PERSON IN ROOM (FEMALE)

New Year's Eve fireworks _____ . . . oh wait, never mind!
                             NOUN

My fireworks show, on the other _____, is the highlight of
                              PART OF THE BODY

the city's _____ New Year's Eve celebrations. Hey, it's totally
         ADJECTIVE

not fair to bring up the Eiffel _____!
                        NOUN

From I LOVE SEATTLE MAD LIBS® • Copyright © 2014 by Price Stern Sloan,
an imprint of Penguin Group (USA) LLC, 345 Hudson Street, New York, NY 10014.

MAD LIBS® is fun to play with friends, but you can also play it by yourself! To begin with, DO NOT look at the story on the page below. Fill in the blanks on this page with the words called for. Then, using the words you have selected, fill in the blank spaces in the story.

Now you've created your own hilarious MAD LIBS® game!

WE ARE THE CHAMPIONS!

NOUN _____

PLURAL NOUN _____

PLURAL NOUN _____

PLURAL NOUN _____

ADJECTIVE _____

NOUN _____

ANIMAL (PLURAL) _____

VERB _____

ADJECTIVE _____

NOUN _____

ADVERB _____

NOUN _____

ADJECTIVE _____

NOUN _____

PLURAL NOUN _____

ADJECTIVE _____

NOUN _____

NOUN _____

MAD LIBS

WE ARE THE CHAMPIONS!

The Seattle Seahawks joined the NFL in 1976 as an expansion

_____ . Since then, the Seahawks have won eight division
  NOUN

_____ and two conference _____ . They are the
  PLURAL NOUN   PLURAL NOUN

only team to have played in both the AFC and NFC Championship

_____ . They also have played in two _____
  PLURAL NOUN   ADJECTIVE

Bowls, most recently Super _____ XLVIII, where they
                                    NOUN

defeated the Denver _____ 43–8 to _____
                         ANIMAL (PLURAL)   VERB

their first title. The Seahawks have some of the most _____
                                                              ADJECTIVE

fans of any NFL team. In fact, Seattle's fans are known as "the

12th _____ ." They _____ hold the Guinness
        NOUN   ADVERB

_____ Record for the most _____ roar from a
  NOUN   ADJECTIVE

crowd. The Seahawks' secondary, called the _____ of Boom,
                                                    NOUN

are some of the most hard-hitting, high-energy _____ you'll
                                                       PLURAL NOUN

ever watch on a football field. And they're kind of hard to miss in those

_____ uniforms of _____ navy, _____
  ADJECTIVE   NOUN   NOUN

green, and gray. Go 'Hawks!

From I LOVE SEATTLE MAD LIBS® • Copyright © 2014 by Price Stern Sloan,
an imprint of Penguin Group (USA) LLC, 345 Hudson Street, New York, NY 10014.

MAD LIBS® is fun to play with friends, but you can also play it by yourself! To begin with, DO NOT look at the story on the page below. Fill in the blanks on this page with the words called for. Then, using the words you have selected, fill in the blank spaces in the story.

Now you've created your own hilarious MAD LIBS® game!

HEY, DON'T FORGET ABOUT US

ANIMAL (PLURAL) _____

PART OF THE BODY _____

NOUN _____

NOUN _____

NOUN _____

ADJECTIVE _____

PLURAL NOUN _____

SAME PLURAL NOUN _____

A PLACE _____

NOUN _____

NOUN _____

PLURAL NOUN _____

MAD LIBS®
HEY, DON'T FORGET
ABOUT US

While the Sea-_____ have recently dominated the
                    ANIMAL (PLURAL)

_____-lines on the sports pages, Seattle has lots of other
PART OF THE BODY

_____ teams that have made news:
     NOUN

• The Seattle Metropolitans—The first American _____
                                                    NOUN

  hockey team to win the Stanley _____ in 1917.
                                      NOUN

• The Seattle SuperSonics—The team made it to the NBA Finals

  for two _____ years in the late 1970s. They lost to the
              ADJECTIVE

  Washington _____ in 1978, but the following year
                 PLURAL NOUN

  they beat the _____ for the championship. The team
                  SAME PLURAL NOUN

  moved to (the) _____ in 2008.
                     A PLACE

• The Seattle Mariners—The city's _____-ball team has
                                        NOUN

  won the American League West _____ three times: in
                                     NOUN

  1995, 1997, and most recently in 2001.

• The Seattle Storm—The city's WNBA team has brought two

  championship _____ to the city, once in 2004 and
                  PLURAL NOUN

  again in 2010.

MAD LIBS® is fun to play with friends, but you can also play it by yourself! To begin with, DO NOT look at the story on the page below. Fill in the blanks on this page with the words called for. Then, using the words you have selected, fill in the blank spaces in the story.

Now you've created your own hilarious MAD LIBS® game!

PIKE PLACE MARKET

ADJECTIVE _____

PLURAL NOUN _____

VERB _____

ADJECTIVE _____

NOUN _____

NOUN _____

TYPE OF LIQUID _____

TYPE OF LIQUID _____

NOUN _____

VERB ENDING IN "ING" _____

ADJECTIVE _____

PLURAL NOUN _____

ADJECTIVE _____

MAD LIBS

PIKE PLACE MARKET

Pike Place Market opened in 1907 and is the most _____
ADJECTIVE

market currently operating in the United States. There are over two

hundred and fifty _____ there, and you can _____
PLURAL NOUN   VERB

just about anything you might want there, like:

- Tourists lining up at the original Starbucks to buy a/an

  _____ iced _____-free vanilla latte.
  ADJECTIVE   NOUN

- Foodies debating whether to buy the fifty-dollars-a-pound

  chunk of _____ or the sixty-dollar bottle of olive
  NOUN

  _____.
  TYPE OF LIQUID

What you *won't* find in Pike Place Market:

- Office workers drinking Folgers _____ and eating
  TYPE OF LIQUID

  Oscar Mayer _____ sandwiches.
  NOUN

- Local teenagers _____ games in a video arcade.
  VERB ENDING IN "ING"

- Store owners selling _____ flowers and frozen
  ADJECTIVE

  _____ to _____ tourists.
  PLURAL NOUN   ADJECTIVE

From I LOVE SEATTLE MAD LIBS® • Copyright © 2014 by Price Stern Sloan,
an imprint of Penguin Group (USA) LLC, 345 Hudson Street, New York, NY 10014.

MAD LIBS® is fun to play with friends, but you can also play it by yourself! To begin with, DO NOT look at the story on the page below. Fill in the blanks on this page with the words called for. Then, using the words you have selected, fill in the blank spaces in the story.

Now you've created your own hilarious MAD LIBS® game!

A BRIEF HISTORY OF SEATTLE

PLURAL NOUN _____

NOUN _____

ADJECTIVE _____

NOUN _____

PLURAL NOUN _____

NUMBER _____

PLURAL NOUN _____

VERB ENDING IN "ING" _____

NOUN _____

PLURAL NOUN _____

NOUN _____

NUMBER _____

MAD LIBS
A BRIEF HISTORY
OF SEATTLE

1851—Two dozen _____ arrive from Portland.
          PLURAL NOUN

1853—Washington Territory founded; Seattle loses out to

Olympia as state _____.
              NOUN

1889—The _____ Fire destroys the heart of the city's
          ADJECTIVE

_____ district.
    NOUN

1910—Washington _____ get the vote,
            PLURAL NOUN

_____ years before they do in the rest of the nation.
    NUMBER

1919—Seattle port _____ initiate the first general
            PLURAL NOUN

strike in the nation.

1940—The Mercer Island Bridge, the world's largest

_____ structure, is built.
    VERB ENDING IN "ING"

1962—The World's _____ opens and runs for six
            NOUN

_____.
    PLURAL NOUN

1999—World Trade _____ protests occur in the city.
            NOUN

2001—A 6.8 earthquake causes more than _____
                            NUMBER

dollars' worth of damage.

MAD LIBS® is fun to play with friends, but you can also play it by yourself! To begin with, DO NOT look at the story on the page below. Fill in the blanks on this page with the words called for. Then, using the words you have selected, fill in the blank spaces in the story.

Now you've created your own hilarious MAD LIBS® game!

STARBUCKS

PLURAL NOUN _____

NOUN _____

ADJECTIVE _____

PERSON IN ROOM (MALE) _____

PLURAL NOUN _____

OCCUPATION _____

ADJECTIVE _____

ADVERB _____

ADJECTIVE _____

PLURAL NOUN _____

PLURAL NOUN _____

NUMBER _____

ADJECTIVE _____

TYPE OF LIQUID _____

ADJECTIVE _____

NOUN _____

MAD LIBS
STARBUCKS

The first Starbucks was opened in Seattle on March 30, 1971, by three

partners who met while they were _____ in college. Originally
                                   PLURAL NOUN

the company was to be called Pequod, after a whaling _____
                                                          NOUN

from the _____ book *Moby-*_____. But this
             ADJECTIVE   PERSON IN ROOM (MALE)

name was vetoed by some of the co-_____. Instead, they
                                    PLURAL NOUN

named the company after the chief _____ on the *Pequod,*
                                      OCCUPATION

Starbuck. In 1987, the original owners sold the Starbucks chain to a/

an _____ employee, and the company _____
      ADJECTIVE   ADVERB

began to expand. At the time of the _____ public offering
                                        ADJECTIVE

in June 1992, Starbucks had grown to 140 _____. The first
                                             PLURAL NOUN

Starbucks located outside of North America opened in Tokyo, Japan,

in 1996. Now there are over twenty thousand _____ in
                                                PLURAL NOUN

_____ countries. At the height of its expansion program,
   NUMBER

Starbucks was opening, on average, two _____ stores
                                           ADJECTIVE

every day. That's an awful lot of _____—make mine a/an
                                   TYPE OF LIQUID

_____ Venti latte with an extra _____.
   ADJECTIVE   NOUN

MAD LIBS® is fun to play with friends, but you can also play it by yourself! To begin with, DO NOT look at the story on the page below. Fill in the blanks on this page with the words called for. Then, using the words you have selected, fill in the blank spaces in the story.

Now you've created your own hilarious MAD LIBS® game!

THE SEATTLE SOUND

PART OF THE BODY _____

NOUN _____

ADJECTIVE _____

NOUN _____

ADJECTIVE _____

ADVERB _____

PLURAL NOUN _____

NOUN _____

TYPE OF FOOD _____

NOUN _____

PERSON IN ROOM (FEMALE) _____

VERB _____

NOUN _____

PLURAL NOUN _____

PLURAL NOUN _____

ADJECTIVE _____

VERB _____

MAD LIBS®

THE SEATTLE SOUND

Music has always been a part of the scene in Seattle, but the city made

music _____-lines when grunge, sometimes referred to as
    PART OF THE BODY

"the Seattle sound," hit the _____-waves in the late 1980s.
                       NOUN

Inspired by _____-core punk, heavy _____,
           ADJECTIVE   NOUN

and _____ rock, grunge is _____ characterized
        ADJECTIVE   ADVERB

by distorted electric _____, fuzz and feedback effects,
                         PLURAL NOUN

and _____-filled lyrics. Some of the bands that captured
           NOUN

that sound and put Seattle on the music map were Nirvana,

Pearl _____, Sound-_____, and
            TYPE OF FOOD   NOUN

_____ in Chains. While you can still _____
PERSON IN ROOM (FEMALE)   VERB

to grunge in Seattle today, the music _____ there has moved
                             NOUN

on, and you're just as likely to hear alt-country _____,
                                    PLURAL NOUN

post-emo song-_____, and _____ folk-pop.
           PLURAL NOUN   ADJECTIVE

_____ on, Seattle!
   VERB

From I LOVE SEATTLE MAD LIBS® • Copyright © 2014 by Price Stern Sloan,
an imprint of Penguin Group (USA) LLC, 345 Hudson Street, New York, NY 10014.

MAD LIBS® is fun to play with friends, but you can also play it by yourself! To begin with, DO NOT look at the story on the page below. Fill in the blanks on this page with the words called for. Then, using the words you have selected, fill in the blank spaces in the story.

Now you've created your own hilarious MAD LIBS® game!

HEY, SEATTLE,
IT'S WASHINGTON CALLING

EXCLAMATION _____

NOUN _____

ADVERB _____

A PLACE _____

NOUN _____

PLURAL NOUN _____

ADJECTIVE _____

SILLY WORD _____

NOUN _____

PERSON IN ROOM (MALE) _____

NOUN _____

ADJECTIVE _____

PLURAL NOUN _____

PLURAL NOUN _____

NOUN _____

TYPE OF LIQUID _____

NOUN _____

MAD LIBS®
HEY, SEATTLE,
IT'S WASHINGTON CALLING

Washington: _____, Seattle. Glad you're part of the
          EXCLAMATION

_____, and you are _____ the first destination
     NOUN   ADVERB

people think of when they think of (the) _____. However,
                                            A PLACE

there's a lot more to the Evergreen _____. Like over 71,000
                                         NOUN

square _____ of _____ wilderness.
        PLURAL NOUN   ADJECTIVE

Seattle: _____, Washington, I get that there's much more
          SILLY WORD

to you than just me, but I'm kind of the star of the _____.
                                                        NOUN

Washington: Well, shall I remind you of the San _____
                                               PERSON IN ROOM (MALE)

Islands, _____ Rainier, and Olympic _____
          NOUN   ADJECTIVE

Park? Thousands of _____ come to Washington every year
                     PLURAL NOUN

to see those _____.
               PLURAL NOUN

Seattle: I know, I know, and I'm glad that we're all part of the

Washington _____, but I'm kind of the highlight. I've got
              NOUN

the restaurants, the museums, and the _____.
                                        TYPE OF LIQUID

Washington: Careful, Seattle, or I may have to get Portland involved

in this _____.
          NOUN

From I LOVE SEATTLE MAD LIBS® • Copyright © 2014 by Price Stern Sloan,
an imprint of Penguin Group (USA) LLC, 345 Hudson Street, New York, NY 10014.

MAD LIBS® is fun to play with friends, but you can also play it by yourself! To begin with, DO NOT look at the story on the page below. Fill in the blanks on this page with the words called for. Then, using the words you have selected, fill in the blank spaces in the story.

Now you've created your own hilarious MAD LIBS® game!

SEATTLE SONS
AND DAUGHTERS

ADJECTIVE _____

PERSON IN ROOM (MALE) _____

PERSON IN ROOM (FEMALE) _____

NOUN _____

PLURAL NOUN _____

PART OF THE BODY _____

PERSON IN ROOM _____

PERSON IN ROOM (FEMALE) _____

ADJECTIVE _____

ANIMAL _____

MAD LIBS
SEATTLE SONS
AND DAUGHTERS

Seattle has lots of famous sons and daughters, such as:

- Paul Allen—cofounder of computer company

  Micro-_____
          ADJECTIVE

- _____ Batali—chef and restaurateur
  PERSON IN ROOM (MALE)

- _____ Brownstein—comedienne and star of TV
  PERSON IN ROOM (FEMALE)

  show *Portlandia*

- Judy Collins—folk _____
                        NOUN

- Bill _____—cofounder of Microsoft
       PLURAL NOUN

- Ben Haggerty (aka Macklemore)—_____-hop artist
                                 PART OF THE BODY

- _____ Hendrix—rock legend
  PERSON IN ROOM

- Gypsy _____ Lee—actress and burlesque star
        PERSON IN ROOM (FEMALE)

- Apolo Ohno—Olympic _____-track speed skater
                     ADJECTIVE

- Adam West—actor, best known for playing _____-man
                                          ANIMAL

  in the 1960s TV show

MAD LIBS® is fun to play with friends, but you can also play it by yourself! To begin with, DO NOT look at the story on the page below. Fill in the blanks on this page with the words called for. Then, using the words you have selected, fill in the blank spaces in the story.

Now you've created your own hilarious MAD LIBS® game!

THE *TWILIGHT* ZONE

PERSON IN ROOM (MALE) _____

ADJECTIVE _____

PLURAL NOUN _____

NOUN _____

ADJECTIVE _____

NOUN _____

NOUN _____

VERB _____

ADJECTIVE _____

VERB ENDING IN "ING" _____

ADJECTIVE _____

VEHICLE _____

NOUN _____

PERSON IN ROOM (FEMALE) _____

NOUN _____

ADJECTIVE _____

ADJECTIVE _____

MAD LIBS

THE *TWILIGHT* ZONE

Whether you're Team Edward or Team _____,

PERSON IN ROOM (MALE)

Seattle is a/an _____ spot to start a tour of some of the

ADJECTIVE

_____ used in the Twilight movies. Hit the _____

PLURAL NOUN   NOUN

and head northwest to the _____ town of Forks—it's just a

ADJECTIVE

three-and-a-half-hour _____ from Seattle. There you can see

NOUN

the famous WELCOME TO FORKS _____ and _____

NOUN   VERB

a selfie to prove you've walked in Bella's _____ Converses.

ADJECTIVE

Next, drop by the Forks _____ Center and take a

VERB ENDING IN "ING"

look at Bella's _____ Chevy pickup _____.

ADJECTIVE   VEHICLE

And don't forget to visit the Swans' _____. However,

NOUN

_____ doesn't really live there, so don't ring the

PERSON IN ROOM (FEMALE)

_____ and expect her to come to the door. Of course you'll

NOUN

need to visit Forks _____ School, where lots of scenes were

ADJECTIVE

filmed. You can show your _____ Spartan spirit (or don't—

ADJECTIVE

Bella never did).

From I LOVE SEATTLE MAD LIBS® • Copyright © 2014 by Price Stern Sloan,
an imprint of Penguin Group (USA) LLC, 345 Hudson Street, New York, NY 10014.

MAD LIBS® is fun to play with friends, but you can also play it by yourself! To begin with, DO NOT look at the story on the page below. Fill in the blanks on this page with the words called for. Then, using the words you have selected, fill in the blank spaces in the story.

Now you've created your own hilarious MAD LIBS® game!

SEATTLE ON-SCREEN

SILLY WORD _____

PERSON IN ROOM _____

NOUN _____

NOUN _____

ADJECTIVE _____

ADJECTIVE _____

PERSON IN ROOM (MALE) _____

VERB _____

ADJECTIVE _____

PERSON IN ROOM (FEMALE) _____

NOUN _____

VERB _____

NOUN _____

VERB _____

NOUN _____

PERSON IN ROOM (MALE) _____

VERB ENDING IN "ING" _____

ADJECTIVE _____

MAD LIBS

SEATTLE ON-SCREEN

_____! My name is _____, and I'll be
SILLY WORD   PERSON IN ROOM

your tour _____ for the Seattle On-Screen movie tour.
NOUN

Our tour today begins at Lake Union. If you look to your left,

you'll see the _____-boat where Sam and Jonah lived in
NOUN

_____ *in Seattle.* Next we'll drop by the Seattle Center,
ADJECTIVE

which played a/an _____ part in the movie *It Happened*
ADJECTIVE

at the World's Fair, starring _____ Presley. As we
PERSON IN ROOM (MALE)

_____ through Belltown, you might recognize scenes
VERB

from *The _____ Baker Boys.* _____ Pfeiffer
ADJECTIVE   PERSON IN ROOM (FEMALE)

earned an Academy _____ for her role in that movie. Let's
NOUN

take a detour to Tacoma and _____ in front of the large
VERB

coffeepot-shaped _____ that appeared in the teen-angst
NOUN

movie _____ *Anything.* And finally, our tour ends with a/
VERB

an _____ at the Triangle Pub, which was featured in *Get*
NOUN

_____. So thanks for _____ the tour,
PERSON IN ROOM (MALE)   VERB ENDING IN "ING"

and we hope to see you again in our _____ city soon!
ADJECTIVE

From I LOVE SEATTLE MAD LIBS® • Copyright © 2014 by Price Stern Sloan,
an imprint of Penguin Group (USA) LLC, 345 Hudson Street, New York, NY 10014.

MAD LIBS® is fun to play with friends, but you can also play it by yourself! To begin with, DO NOT look at the story on the page below. Fill in the blanks on this page with the words called for. Then, using the words you have selected, fill in the blank spaces in the story.

Now you've created your own hilarious MAD LIBS® game!

A VISIT TO OLYMPIC NATIONAL PARK

VERB _____

NOUN _____

VERB ENDING IN "ING" _____

PLURAL NOUN _____

ADJECTIVE _____

NOUN _____

VEHICLE _____

NOUN _____

VERB _____

PLURAL NOUN _____

PLURAL NOUN _____

VERB _____

VERB ENDING IN "ING" _____

PLURAL NOUN _____

ADJECTIVE _____

A PLACE _____

VERB _____

MAD LIBS®
A VISIT TO
OLYMPIC NATIONAL PARK

Husband: I'm so glad that we visited Seattle and will have some

time to _____ in Olympic National _____.
　　　　　　　VERB　　　　　　　　　　　　　　　　　NOUN

Wife: Are you sure we're _____ in the right
　　　　　　　　　　　　　　VERB ENDING IN "ING"

direction? I haven't seen any _____ for the park.
　　　　　　　　　　　　　　PLURAL NOUN

Husband: Did you know that the park is one of the few

_____ parks in the West with a/an _____ beach?
ADJECTIVE　　　　　　　　　　　　　　　　　　　　　NOUN

Wife: I just don't trust the GPS in this _____. What did
　　　　　　　　　　　　　　　　　　　　　VEHICLE

you do with the _____ map? I want to take a look at it.
　　　　　　　　NOUN

Husband: We can _____ the Hoh or Sol Duc
　　　　　　　　　　　　VERB

_____, fish for _____ in the Dickey River, and
PLURAL NOUN　　　　　　PLURAL NOUN

_____ on Lake Crescent.
VERB

Wife: Well, we aren't going to do any of that unless you start

_____ in the direction of the park.
VERB ENDING IN "ING"

Husband: And just think of the _____ we can have in
　　　　　　　　　　　　　　　　　PLURAL NOUN

the _____ meadows.
　　　ADJECTIVE

Wife: I hate to tell you this, but we're heading toward (the)

_____. Pull over right now. I'm going to _____.
A PLACE　　　　　　　　　　　　　　　　　　　　　VERB

MAD LIBS® is fun to play with friends, but you can also play it by yourself! To begin with, DO NOT look at the story on the page below. Fill in the blanks on this page with the words called for. Then, using the words you have selected, fill in the blank spaces in the story.

Now you've created your own hilarious MAD LIBS® game!

SEATTLE
WEATHER REPORT

PERSON IN ROOM _____

EXCLAMATION _____

NOUN _____

ADJECTIVE _____

PLURAL NOUN _____

ADJECTIVE _____

PART OF THE BODY (PLURAL) _____

PLURAL NOUN _____

ADJECTIVE _____

PLURAL NOUN _____

NOUN _____

NOUN _____

SILLY WORD _____

PLURAL NOUN _____

ADJECTIVE _____

ADJECTIVE _____

MAD LIBS®
SEATTLE
WEATHER REPORT

Hi, this is _____ with your seven-day Seattle forecast.
                    PERSON IN ROOM

    Monday: _____! Can you believe we're actually going to
                    EXCLAMATION

see the _____ today? Hope you can all cope with some
              NOUN

_____ sunshine.
    ADJECTIVE

    Tuesday: But don't worry, the _____ and rain will
                                      PLURAL NOUN

return. We can look forward to _____ hair and wet
                                      ADJECTIVE

_____ all day today.
PART OF THE BODY (PLURAL)

    Wednesday: Keep your _____ handy, because this
                              PLURAL NOUN

weather isn't going anywhere. Ahhhh, life in _____Seattle!
                                                  ADJECTIVE

    Thursday: Hmmm . . . It looks like the rain will stop today, and

we can expect sunny _____. Get your _____-glasses
                          PLURAL NOUN   NOUN

and suntan _____ ready! _____!
                  NOUN   SILLY WORD

    Friday: The rain _____ will be back in full force, and
                            PLURAL NOUN

life will go back to _____.
                          ADJECTIVE

And then we'll have two _____ days of rain, so you know
                              ADJECTIVE

what that means, Seattleites—the weekend is here!

MAD LIBS® is fun to play with friends, but you can also play it by yourself! To begin with, DO NOT look at the story on the page below. Fill in the blanks on this page with the words called for. Then, using the words you have selected, fill in the blank spaces in the story.

Now you've created your own hilarious MAD LIBS® game!

YOU KNOW YOU'RE FROM SEATTLE IF YOU . . .

NUMBER _____

TYPE OF LIQUID _____

PLURAL NOUN _____

VERB ENDING IN "ING" _____

ADJECTIVE _____

COLOR _____

ADJECTIVE _____

PLURAL NOUN _____

VERB ENDING IN "ING" _____

ADJECTIVE _____

ADJECTIVE _____

NOUN _____

ADJECTIVE _____

TYPE OF LIQUID _____

NOUN _____

ARTICLE OF CLOTHING _____

MAD LIBS®
YOU KNOW YOU'RE FROM SEATTLE IF YOU...

- Know more than _____ words to describe a cup of
  NUMBER

  _____
  TYPE OF LIQUID

- Obey all traffic _____, except "keep right unless
  PLURAL NOUN

  _____ "
  VERB ENDING IN "ING"

- Often find yourself standing at a/an _____ street corner
  ADJECTIVE

  in the rain waiting for the light to go to _____
  COLOR

- Are shocked by a/an _____ weather forecast
  ADJECTIVE

- Go to a bar and sit at a table. Waiters are easier to handle than

  _____ .
  PLURAL NOUN

- Consider _____ an indoor sport. And that's why
  VERB ENDING IN "ING"

  you never have a/an _____ tan
  ADJECTIVE

- Feel _____ throwing an aluminum _____
  ADJECTIVE   NOUN

  into the trash

- Get _____ when a store doesn't carry your favorite
  ADJECTIVE

  brand of bottled _____
  TYPE OF LIQUID

- Design your Halloween _____ to fit under a rain-
  NOUN

  _____
  ARTICLE OF CLOTHING

MAD LIBS® is fun to play with friends, but you can also play it by yourself! To begin with, DO NOT look at the story on the page below. Fill in the blanks on this page with the words called for. Then, using the words you have selected, fill in the blank spaces in the story.

Now you've created your own hilarious MAD LIBS® game!

WHICH SEATTLE NEIGHBORHOOD ARE YOU?

PLURAL NOUN _____

NOUN _____

PART OF THE BODY _____

NOUN _____

ADJECTIVE _____

PLURAL NOUN _____

ADJECTIVE _____

VERB ENDING IN "ING" _____

PLURAL NOUN _____

ADJECTIVE _____

PART OF THE BODY _____

A PLACE _____

PLURAL NOUN _____

NOUN _____

COLOR _____

ADVERB _____

PLURAL NOUN _____

PLURAL NOUN _____

MAD LIBS®
WHICH SEATTLE
NEIGHBORHOOD ARE YOU?

- Fremont: You don't like wearing _____, but have been
  _____PLURAL NOUN

  known to wear a/an _____ on your _____.
  _____NOUN_____PART OF THE BODY

- Central District: You have a major _____ crisis. Some days
  _____NOUN

  you're _____ and street-smart; other days you look like an
  _____ADJECTIVE

  ad for Urban _____.
  _____PLURAL NOUN

- Belltown: You're _____ until five o'clock, but after that it's
  _____ADJECTIVE

  all about _____ the _____.
  _____VERB ENDING IN "ING"_____PLURAL NOUN

- Ballard: You are the picture of _____, or at least you are in
  _____ADJECTIVE

  your own _____. But on the weekends, you turn into
  _____PART OF THE BODY

  a cast member from (the) _____ *Shore*.
  _____A PLACE

- Pioneer Square: You bore people with stories of how _____
  _____PLURAL NOUN

  used to be. Change the _____, please!
  _____NOUN

- Queen Anne: Some people think you're stuck in a/an _____
  _____COLOR

  tower, and you _____ are. But it's worth it for the great
  _____ADVERB

  brunch _____.
  _____PLURAL NOUN

Figure out where you belong and start packing those _____!
  _____PLURAL NOUN

From I LOVE SEATTLE MAD LIBS® • Copyright © 2014 by Price Stern Sloan,
an imprint of Penguin Group (USA) LLC, 345 Hudson Street, New York, NY 10014.

MAD LIBS® is fun to play with friends, but you can also play it by yourself! To begin with, DO NOT look at the story on the page below. Fill in the blanks on this page with the words called for. Then, using the words you have selected, fill in the blank spaces in the story.

Now you've created your own hilarious MAD LIBS® game!

WHAT SHOULD WE DO WHILE WE'RE HERE?

NUMBER _____

NOUN _____

ADJECTIVE _____

ADVERB _____

ANIMAL _____

ADJECTIVE _____

PERSON IN ROOM _____

PLURAL NOUN _____

VERB _____

TYPE OF FOOD _____

PLURAL NOUN _____

ADJECTIVE _____

ADVERB _____

ADJECTIVE _____

TYPE OF LIQUID _____

PLURAL NOUN _____

VERB ENDING IN "ING" _____

MAD LIBS®
WHAT SHOULD WE DO
WHILE WE'RE HERE?

Tourist #1: Okay, we have _____ hours in Seattle.
<u>NUMBER</u>

What do you want to do? I definitely want to visit the Seattle

_____ Museum to see some _____ art.
<u>NOUN</u>   <u>ADJECTIVE</u>

Tourist #2: I _____ want to visit the Seattle Aquarium
<u>ADVERB</u>

and see the giant Pacific _____.
<u>ANIMAL</u>

Tourist #1: Okay, but after that can we check out the

_____ work of _____ Chihuly? I promise I won't
<u>ADJECTIVE</u>   <u>PERSON IN ROOM</u>

touch any of the _____.
<u>PLURAL NOUN</u>

Tourist #2: And we've got to _____ the Washington
<u>VERB</u>

Park Arboretum since the Japanese _____ trees are in
<u>TYPE OF FOOD</u>

bloom.

Tourist #1: Let's rent some _____ and bike there.
<u>PLURAL NOUN</u>

Tourist #2: And a _____ farmers' market.
<u>ADJECTIVE</u>

Tourist #1: And we _____ need to drop by the
<u>ADVERB</u>

_____ Starbucks for a cup of _____.
<u>ADJECTIVE</u>   <u>TYPE OF LIQUID</u>

Tourist #2: We only have forty-eight _____. We better
<u>PLURAL NOUN</u>

get _____!
<u>VERB ENDING IN "ING"</u>

MAD LIBS® is fun to play with friends, but you can also play it by yourself! To begin with, DO NOT look at the story on the page below. Fill in the blanks on this page with the words called for. Then, using the words you have selected, fill in the blank spaces in the story.

Now you've created your own hilarious MAD LIBS® game!

BE TRUE TO YOUR SCHOOL

NUMBER _____

ADJECTIVE _____

NOUN _____

PLURAL NOUN _____

PLURAL NOUN _____

ADJECTIVE _____

NOUN _____

PLURAL NOUN _____

COLOR _____

ANIMAL _____

ADJECTIVE _____

PLURAL NOUN _____

LETTER OF THE ALPHABET_____

NOUN _____

ANIMAL (PLURAL) _____

MAD☺LIBS®
BE TRUE TO YOUR SCHOOL

Seattle is home to more than _____ colleges and universities.
NUMBER

- Antioch University—A/An _____, not-for-profit
  ADJECTIVE

  school. Many of Antioch's students study conversation and

  _____ management.
  NOUN

- Art Institute of Seattle—Founded in 1946. _____ at the
  PLURAL NOUN

  institute can study design, media _____, fashion, and
  PLURAL NOUN

  _____ arts.
  ADJECTIVE

- Cornish College of the Arts—The mission of the _____ is
  NOUN

  to teach students who want to become practicing _____.
  PLURAL NOUN

- Le Cordon _____: Learn how to cook everything from
  COLOR

  _____ à l'orange to _____ pastry.
  ANIMAL   ADJECTIVE

- Seattle University—The university is ranked among the top-ten

  _____ in the West.
  PLURAL NOUN

- University of Washington—Known as _____-Dub,
  LETTER OF THE ALPHABET

  the university is famous for its School of _____ and is
  NOUN

  the home of the _____, a championship football team.
  ANIMAL (PLURAL)

MAD LIBS® is fun to play with friends, but you can also play it by yourself! To begin with, DO NOT look at the story on the page below. Fill in the blanks on this page with the words called for. Then, using the words you have selected, fill in the blank spaces in the story.

Now you've created your own hilarious MAD LIBS® game!

PORTLAND CALLING

EXCLAMATION _____

NOUN _____

VERB _____

ADJECTIVE _____

VERB ENDING IN "ING" _____

SILLY WORD _____

NOUN _____

VERB _____

VERB ENDING IN "ING" _____

NOUN _____

ADJECTIVE _____

PART OF THE BODY _____

ADJECTIVE _____

SILLY WORD _____

TYPE OF LIQUID _____

SAME TYPE OF LIQUID _____

PART OF THE BODY _____

VERB ENDING IN "ING" _____

MAD LIBS®
PORTLAND CALLING

Portland: _____, Seattle! So you think you're the
_{EXCLAMATION}

_____ of the Northwest? Well, _____ again.
_{NOUN}   _{VERB}

Your _____ neighbor to the south is _____
           _{ADJECTIVE}   _{VERB ENDING IN "ING"}

at your door.

Seattle: _____, Portland! You certainly have delusions
                _{SILLY WORD}

of _____. First of all, more people_____ in my
      _{NOUN}   _{VERB}

city limits.

Portland: Well, you might have a few thousand more residents,

but all of them are usually _____ in traffic jams.
                                _{VERB ENDING IN "ING"}

Seattle: And what's that body of _____ you're on? Oh,
                                      _{NOUN}

it's just a/an _____ river. I, on the other _____,
                _{ADJECTIVE}   _{PART OF THE BODY}

am located on the _____ Pacific Ocean.
                      _{ADJECTIVE}

Portland: _____! And while you think you are the
                _{SILLY WORD}

King of _____, we've got some pretty awesome
             _{TYPE OF LIQUID}

_____-houses, and we whup your _____
_{SAME TYPE OF LIQUID}   _{PART OF THE BODY}

when it comes to beer.

Tacoma: Blah, blah, blah, you two keep _____.
                                                  _{VERB ENDING IN "ING"}

From I LOVE SEATTLE MAD LIBS® • Copyright © 2014 by Price Stern Sloan,
an imprint of Penguin Group (USA) LLC, 345 Hudson Street, New York, NY 10014.

MAD LIBS® is fun to play with friends, but you can also play it by yourself! To begin with, DO NOT look at the story on the page below. Fill in the blanks on this page with the words called for. Then, using the words you have selected, fill in the blank spaces in the story.

Now you've created your own hilarious MAD LIBS® game!

SEATTLE DOS AND DON'TS

ADJECTIVE _____

PLURAL NOUN _____

NOUN _____

NUMBER _____

NOUN _____

NOUN _____

ANIMAL _____

ADJECTIVE _____

PLURAL NOUN _____

ADJECTIVE _____

VERB ENDING IN "ING" _____

TYPE OF LIQUID _____

NOUN _____

ADJECTIVE _____

MAD LIBS

SEATTLE DOS AND DON'TS

Seattle has some pretty _____ laws. Here are some of the
                          ADJECTIVE

_____ that Seattleites must abide by:
PLURAL NOUN

- You may not carry a concealed _____ that is over
                                      NOUN

  _____ feet in length.
       NUMBER

- You may not spit on a city _____.
                                  NOUN

- You may not set fire to another person's _____ without
                                                 NOUN

  prior permission.

- You may not carry a/an _____—bowl or aquarium on
                              ANIMAL

  a bus because the sound of _____ water may disturb
                                  ADJECTIVE

  other _____.
        PLURAL NOUN

- You may not display a hypnotized or supposedly _____
                                                      ADJECTIVE

  person in a store window.

And don't ever get caught _____ a cup of Stumptown
                              VERB ENDING IN "ING"

_____. However, you can buy, sell, and smoke
   TYPE OF LIQUID

_____. So let's get_____!
      NOUN   ADJECTIVE

From I LOVE SEATTLE MAD LIBS® • Copyright © 2014 by Price Stern Sloan,
an imprint of Penguin Group (USA) LLC, 345 Hudson Street, New York, NY 10014.

This book is published by

PSS!
PRICE STERN SLOAN

whose other splendid titles include
such literary classics as

Ad Lib Mad Libs®

All I Want for Christmas Is Mad Libs®

Best of Mad Libs®

Camp Daze Mad Libs®

Christmas Carol Mad Libs®

Christmas Fun Mad Libs®

Cool Mad Libs®

Dance Mania Mad Libs®

Dear Valentine Letters Mad Libs®

Diva Girl Mad Libs®

Dude, Where's My Mad Libs®

Easter Eggstravaganza Mad Libs®

Escape from Detention Mad Libs®

Family Tree Mad Libs®

Girls Just Wanna Have Mad Libs®

Gobble Gobble Mad Libs®

Goofy Mad Libs®

Grab Bag Mad Libs®

Graduation Mad Libs®

Grand Slam Mad Libs®

Hanukkah Mad Libs®

Happily Ever Mad Libs®

Happy Birthday Mad Libs®

Haunted Mad Libs®

Holly, Jolly Mad Libs®

Hot Off the Presses Mad Libs®

Kid Libs Mad Libs®

Letters from Camp Mad Libs®

Luck of the Mad Libs®

Mad About Animals Mad Libs®

Mad About Mad Libs®

Mad Libs® Forever

Mad Libs® for President

Mad Libs® from Outer Space

Mad Libs® in Love

Mad Libs® on the Road

Mad Mad Mad Mad Mad Libs®

Mad Scientist Mad Libs®

Monster Mad Libs®

More Best of Mad Libs®

Night of the Living Mad Libs®

Ninjas Mad Libs®

Off-the-Wall Mad Libs®

The Original #1 Mad Libs®

P. S. I Love Mad Libs®

Peace, Love, and Mad Libs®

Pirates Mad Libs®

Rock 'n' Roll Mad Libs®

Slam Dunk Mad Libs®

Sleepover Party Mad Libs®

Sooper Dooper Mad Libs®

Spooky Mad Libs®

Spy Mad Libs®

Straight "A" Mad Libs®

Totally Pink Mad Libs®

Undead Mad Libs®

Upside Down Mad Libs®

Vacation Fun Mad Libs®

Winter Games Mad Libs®

You've Got Mad Libs®

and many, many more!

Mad Libs® are available wherever books are sold.